Seeds of Secrets

Universal Lessons from Love, Loss, and Life

By Kathleen Byron Etzel

ISBN: 978-93-6354-351-5

First Edition: 2025
Rs. 200/-

Cyberwit.net
HIG 45 Kaushambi Kunj, Kalindipuram
Allahabad - 211011 (U.P.) India
http://www.cyberwit.net
E-mail: info@cyberwit.net

Printed at Repro India Limited.

Contents

Night is Done

Oh, let the words come to me
Fleeting, though, they may be
On the tip of my tongue
"Go!"
Our night is done
For among the layered woven lies
Love must survive

Snowy Shores

Beyond snowy shores
A sullen gull pecks remains
Of yesterday's news
From
A muse
Of love gone by
Yet here today
Only gratitude for
All that may
Welcome home
A brand new day

North to South

There in the waves
The answers
I seek
And now I see
You be mine
And
I be yours
From East to West
And North to South
Lips to mouth
For ever more

Future

Dream with me
Our future I see
Do you too?
Love me more each day
Tomorrow's better than before
Because I'll love you even more

Do You Know

Do you know?
Do
You
Know?

Why

Why
No, let me ask
Finally at last

She be Stormy

Sunday mornin'
The weather,
She be stormy
Monday evening -
The clouds
They be rollin' on
Tuesday noon-
I'm still mourning-
My baby she be
Gone, oh too soon

Clowns

Button downs
Make me frown
When all around
Are a bunch of clowns

Already Gone

How can she leave you
If you've already gone?

Write

Where can I write out of sight
From the winds that break
My waiting life

Floodgates

Let the floodgates begin of eternal sin,
Not mine, but yours
You hide to procure
While lying in wait
For all you can take
Year after year
All the while,
I'm blindly here

Ode to Cornelia

Yes, my best friend
Through the years, many times
You asked
I said no
To something I felt
But dared not say
For in you - adventure, discovery, laughter
Oh my God, laughter

Example?
Dragging your mattress up six flights
Losing our grip
Only to watch it fall
Tumble really
We laughed with hysteria
As it crashed
To the ground so far below
A metaphor for all to come
And God knows
Already had befallen
Tragically before

You picked me up when no one could
You gave me truth
Reason to believe
When no one could
Reason to believe
What?
Yes I could love again

How do you tell someone everything anytime?
Every detail?
This was our truth - equally
You didn't go
I did

I see it was me
I left
Only now I do know
What I didn't know
That was the last time
After so many years
The last time I would see you
I saw you
I still see you clearly

Laying there
Sound asleep
Your own broken-hearted hand of fate
Hurting you
Killing you inside and out
Love left
Our symbiotic pain

It's only now
I see what I failed to perceive
My friend
My very dearest friend
In the eternal evening light
When I think of you effortlessly
Often, always
All we've done
All we did

Laughter through the poignant years
Ecstasy ending in despair

Somehow though, the explanation's not mine
Those years mean more than any other decade

Cornelia, I love you
I've never said it before
But here you go
You always wanted me
To say
I love you
And I do

From Jerry to Bob
Magically lighting our manor
On the mountain
With all
The strange journeys we've shared
Re-igniting life
This you gave me
During our time of
Joint existence
A time
The time
When I could love
We could love
With an unbridled God-given
Free-spirited
Love

In you, I see
A life, your brilliant life
Our life – ease

But why?
Tell me
Help me
Yours –
Your being extinguished too soon
You must now know?

Old friend
In the afterlife, dube
Ready to hand
You'll let me know

My journey
Not at its end
Not yet I don't think
Did you know?

No matter for
I'll see you waiting
When I ultimately
We all inevitably
Pass through the door

Walk we will
Till evening light and beyond
Greeting the forever dawn
Once again carefree
But this time
Pain-free
From love
Young love
That captivated you
And God knows me

Mother Time

Western winds blew me to you
Eastern moons said yes I do
Mother Time took all we knew
Sent us sailing with much ado

Now I wonder – no, I ponder
What's out yonder?

Look

Do you stop and look?
Or
Do you stop and watch?

Abyss

A long short time ago
I sure can't remember
I traveled down some road
And now it's mid November

Looking for some kind of sign
To jog my mind
When there behind
No, wait straight ahead
Is the smoldering ember
From that long ago, September
When I lost my head
And set forth on a path that lead
To the abyss
But now I miss my golden glow
So I must go

Unification

Rather than suffer in single solidarity
Uplift with unlimited unification

Evermore

When the beginning begins
The end rescinds
But nothing like before
Fore until another
The door be closed
And answer not nevermore
But for now, let the floods of warmth
Soothe our soul
So much to say
But I can't, not yet
Someday evermore

Mind Travel

Do you dabble
In mind travel?
If so-
Where do you
Go?
If you don't mind,
I'd love
To know

Free

I want to be free
Free from
Free to
Isn't life as simple as that?

Free to be the beautiful being
I was when born
Before
Living fractured moments of
Flowing joy-
Now stripped away

I want to be free
Free from fear,
From guilt
And worry

Free to love
Free to feel peace
Harmony
To travel within my soul to
Parts of the world
To me, yet known

Free to breath
Free to leave the life I lead

Integrity

Who cares what you think
Whether they wear blue or pink
Or scribble prophetic words with chalk or ink
The best medicine anyone can prescribe
Is mining within your tribe
And only feel your vibe
With honest integrity that helps one survive
The angry bee hive
Of man's divide

Wonderment

Ours is an unvarnished, passionate moment
Forever encapsulated in
A memory of impassioned intertwinement

Seeds of Secrets

Seeds of secrets planted all around me
Singing to the shadows of my mind

Create

Create the environment you want
Within the environment, you have

Decide

It was in that moment
I decided my fate

Intoxicating

It doesn't have to be her
But
It was that moment
Those moments
That were so intoxicating,
Enduring
And shall be
Unapologetically
For all eternity
It doesn't have to be her
Or
Does it?

Sing

Bring me to
A land where they can sing
Joyful words
The people, their minds rejoicing
And children run free

Shadows

Singing shadows
Of sun reaching
Beyond tomorrow's
Bury segments
Of your heart

Threads of Tears

Fleeting memories
Threads of tears
Life with peers
From here to there
Throughout the years
Always always love
We share

Ripples of Wind

Ripples of wind
Across our skin
Begins
Our Divide -
Did we sin
As parting waves
Behave rules of tarnished love
Yet where might we be
If only we could see
No, imagine
A brilliant setting sun
And tranquil seas

Of Another World

If I live not of this
World
But of another –
Would you still love me?

www.ingramcontent.com/pod-product-compliance
Lightning Source LLC
LaVergne TN
LVHW041003150826
845672LV00002B/850

* 9 7 8 9 3 6 3 5 4 3 5 1 5 *